mind full
of memories

Róisín Taylor

Cover design by Katarina Nskvsky
Formatting and designs by Daiana Vanesa Marchesi
Map illustration by Daniela Jarrín Sánchez

ISBN: 979-8-4533-5381-1

For you who believe

Contents

Preface

This may not be your "normal" book of poetry - I never did like to do things the way you should. I may not follow trending themes, or delve too deeply into heightened emotions; my dream for this book is to paint a world of adventures, for anyone to join. It flows through time, my time, as each soul-changing venture took place leading me (us) up to my current challenge that is London life!

I've always been a bit of a wandering soul. At 17 I flew the nest and lived in various places dotted along the west coast of my beautiful home that is Ireland. The longest I've stayed anywhere is four years, and by then I felt I had stayed two years too many! So out came my wings and off I set for something - somewhere - new.

The summer of 2009 was my first major adventure, when my Father and I took to the roads of Europe on our fully loaded, burnt orange, 1999 Honda Varadero - or 'Varrie' - as we called her. This five-week trip of 8,000 miles (12,875 km) and truly magnificent landscapes is what awakened my soul to adventure. I was hooked after that trip; my feet could no longer settle and my mind became a whirlwind of dreamings.

Our journey together will start with this adventure, and from there we shall dance upon the wind from Ireland to

Prague, South-East Asia to Sweden, and from the glorious mountains of Nepal to my current home in the UK.

This collection of inner workings, musings, thoughts and feelings will take you on a journey like no other...but only if you set your imagination free long enough; allow your soul to dance along with mine. Do you dare?

To all ye who wander,
Ye who call yourselves 'lost souls',
Walk with me a while
On this vast, twisted path.

Its direction -
Its destination -
Is yet unknown;
The way is fluid and obscured,
Found only when stumbled upon.

I ask ye of guarded hearts,
To loosen that grip just a little
In order to feel the
Glorious
Freedom
In being so lost.

To enjoy the fear
Of not being in control of
Every. Little. Thing.
To allow the air to guide you.

Ye with souls of nurture
And hearts of nature,
Dance along this path with me -
Let us give plenty
To the laws of attraction.

– Ye who wander

Exploring Europa

For a little over five weeks
During the summer of 2009,
We took to the road;
Bike loaded to the max
And kitted with makeshift backrest
To save my spine
From constant connection
With topbox and metal.

Sometimes, I disappear into
Those memories
So fondly,
With a slight smile and
Glazed over eyes;
I am back on 'Varrie',
Perched behind you,
Who is bent over the engine and dials.

We hardly argued,
I do not recall us
Ever with raised voices
Towards each other -
Perhaps a few scattered quiet days
When tired bodies
And over stimulated minds
Could no longer make space
For discussion.

We worked well
As a team;
You would become frustrated
With some form of gadget
From time to time,

And I would remind you
Of the art of breathing -
Together we learned how to
Solve the issues
Only to laugh about them later
Over dinner and wine.

There was one...confusion
Between us,
You remember, I'm sure;
That time,
Outside Venice,
When you spoke to me
With sleep-filled voice,
Reminding me to turn off the cool air;
Only for you to wake -
Near cooked -
In the middle of the night,
Disbelief upon your face,
Adamant that you spoke
Not those words!

We may have been close to a fight then,
I suppose,
If it hadn't been so damn funny!
But for five weeks of constant
You and me -
Me and you -
With one small misunderstanding -
Now hilarious -
Only adding to the whole story,
Solidifying our relationship.

Róisín Taylor

Allowing us to better understand
Our ticks and humour,
Making it easier
To dance around drama
So that we could enjoy
The ever changing view.

– Father & Daughter

We should have been three
And two metal steeds
Setting out on our astonishing
Road trip,
But life happens;
You couldn't make it -
This time.

Perhaps it was fate making
Her statement
Knowing all too well
How it would play out;
Saving you both
From the headaches
Of the inevitable clashing.

Too similar,
And yet
Profoundly different -
Life and fate conspired together
In order to keep you both
Sane.

– Life and Fate

Your quaint villages
Tucked into hidden valleys,
Embraced by your protective
Yet gentle hills
And golden pastures ready for harvest.

Your sand-stone dwellings
And red-tiled rooftops
Paint exquisite sights.
Your mouth-watering dishes
And smooth, rounded wine,
Both undeniably satisfying and
Dangerously morish.

Your delicate cities
Of romantic soul
And timeless structures
Filled my camera with memories,
My eyes with wonder
And my heart with a softness
For your attention to detail.

Your blooming poppies,
Like crimson droplets of blood
Splattered amongst
Fields of gold,
Blurring as we fly by.

Your wonderous mountains
Upon invisible lines,
Looming above, around
And ahead;
Grandiose and spectacular,

Still and powerful,
Strikingly beautiful,
Yet icy cold.

We peer at you in awe,
Breathing every last drop
Of you in
Before entering the tunnel,
Burrowed in between worlds
To enter into a new.

– Falling for France

We wandered in circles
For decades
In the ever soaring heat,
Clad in heavy clothing made
To protect us from gravel,
Causing us to melt and fade
As we searched for St Mark's Square.

But your canals lead us astray,
Your markings leave us dizzy
Causing tempers to rise
Along with the afternoon sun.

I sit and contemplate
Your green, murky waters;
Watch as the black and white stripes
Work the gondolas
Filled with smiling faces,
Who are dressed appropriately
For such heat!

Pointed in the right direction -
Finally -
We stumbled foggily to your
Famous square…
And though you are indeed quite pretty,
I must admit;
I found your winding, narrow streets,
Your labyrinths of water
And the coolness of your shadows,
Much more captivating
To explore.

— *Lost in Venice*

Ancient city of Gods and stone,
Cobbled streets
And mighty quarters
Upon the rising mound,
Reaching out for the clear sky
To bring it closer to their heavenly realm.

The very air does
Waver and swirl -
I melt atop
The crumbling pillars
And time smoothened statues;
The unforgiving sun
Transforming my skin from
Pale to rose
And yours from
Olive to brown
With every passing moment.

But time feels irrelevant here,
As we stand within history
And witness it flourish
And fall;
Looking out upon this hazy city -
That spreads for miles around -
Adapting and changing,
And yet
Ever embracing its
Enduring stacks and carvings;
Creating an agelessness future
From a city moulded from history.

— *The Heavens of Athens*

It is strange to set one's
Thoughts to it;
The crushing fact that
Of those we visited
In the stunning land of
Sleeping gods,
Two have since parted
From this world;
One suddenly
And the other tragically...
Though,
For the life of me,
I cannot tell you
Which belongs to who,
Nor
Why it had to be.
That is the fragility of life,
And time will always have her way.

— Alan & Andrew Harding RIP

Our introduction, of rather
Dramatic displays on an
Otherwise calm ferry -
Your phone call causing
Fits of rage by some
And shouts in your defense
From others -
Who knew using a phone
On a boat
Could cause such a scene?

With this taste of unexpected
And confused discomfort,
We entered Turkey
On edge
And unable to explain
Or to be explained to;
Just pointing and gesturing
And frantic faces.

You moved not an inch
For the remainder of that
Journey -
Statue-like with piercing eyes
That scan for further hostilities.
You tell me to sleep;
But I would have slept better
Had I been on a rollercoaster,
My body being tossed from side to side
With screams torn from my lips...

So instead I close my eyes
And listen to the sounds

Of a tongue so forgein from my own,
Relishing the unfamiliarity;
Learning the dance of this
New sound -
Distracting myself from the unease.

A palpable sigh of relief
For the land
When it finally came into view.

– Entering Turkey

Although the hotel owner sought
To keep me
And insisted on joining us
At dinner,
I cannot say a bad word
About this place;
For the wonderful receptionist
Abandoned her ship
To show us her
Spectacular city,
Of majestic mosques
Of blue and gold -
Such detail in every crevice.

Her eyes shining with
Heart-warming pride
As she leads us by hand
To palaces, parks
And hidden cafes
With the world's most
Sweetest juices.

Sipping tea from narrow glasses
As we stare out
Across the waters
At the alluringly tempting continent
Of Asia.

We drink it all in
With wonder and gratitude,
For this beautiful gift that
Our Wonder Woman has given us.

Heads full of sights
And tales;
It's of no surprise
That come the time
Of our reluctant departure,
We forgot to take our passports!

– Istanbul's Wonder Woman

Two hours from the border
We realised our unfathomable error;
Our pocket-sized booklets
Of identification
Forgotten
Left behind in the glorious Istanbul.

On the verge of exploding
With frustration
You ready yourself
For the four-hour journey back -
Telling me to wait
At this remote filling station
Alone.

That is when Mustaf entered our lives,
Coming to our aid
Having witnessed our distress playing upon
Our faces;
Repeating "no problem"
After many attempts at explaining
Our predicament,
Causing your agitation to grow.

He vanished into his red and white store,
Returning moments later -
A lifetime for our frantic hearts -
Beaming his infectious smile
"No problem," he proclaims,
Much to our confusion;
This amazing stranger had -
The gods only knows how -
Arranged for our passports

To board a bus
Heading for the border;
A little adventure of their own.

I sense your entire soul
Ease
With a relief only you can know -
Even while mixed
With a tinge of disbelief.

Embracing Mustaf with gratitude
And laughter,
We pray to invisible gods
That all is as it seems.

Taking chance by the arm
We wave our thanks and farewells
To Mustaf
As we set off to meet our
Identities
At the border into Bulgaria.

– Border-Line Issues

Much needed was this time
Of rest;
A week relaxing by the warm,
Blue waters -
Home of the Black Sea.

Spending time with somewhat-missed family
On vacation,
Sipping Bacardi
And laughing merrily.

Exploring the Old City
When we felt our souls
yearn for more adventure -
And avoiding the alluring mayhem
Of Sunny Beach;
Overcrowded with alcohol-soaked
And sunburnt bodies.

A week to let Varrie sleep,
A well-deserved slumber
After weeks of never ending
Horizons
Demanding to be sought.

We plan our route,
We eat and swim and stroll;
Taking our sweet time
As time sweetly allows
Our saddle-sore butts
To rest.

– By the Black Sea

Róisín Taylor

The twisting bends,
The winding, snake-like
Roads
Creeping up into vibrant green
Covered 'moontans'-
As we took to calling you.

Rivers bursting with life,
In a hurry to reach their constant
Destination;
White and blue and grey;
They flow through
Their polished beds
Within the gaping valleys,
Of your perfectly voluptuous
Curves of protection.

The road at your feet
Full of stops and starts
With the people buzzing away,
Fixing and mending
At supposed random.

But up here,
Within your dense vegetation
Of deep and lively hues
And the subtle browns of your rock,
Nature surrounds us
In a loving embrace
As upon you,
We delightfully roam.

– Roaming Romania

Your stunning architecture left us
Hungry for more;
For every delicate,
And intricate detail
Etched upon your stony
Structures.

From your 3D murals
And life-like figures -
Whose eyes do follow
And see -
To your chaotic cathedrals,
Every inch
Covered in ancient carvings;
To be discovered again and again.

Your refreshing waters
By the steps,
A welcoming respite
From the pressing heat.

A city carved from history
By talent and might;
Indeed, dearest Budapest,
You left us speechless
And in awe
Of your creative beauty.

– Dear Budapest

Surprising that it took so long,
For you to really explode,
Surprising still
That it was not directed
Towards the SatNav!
Alas, it was our little devices
Which allowed us to yap
Whilst zipping through time
And space
Who bore the brunt of your rage

To this day
You still wonder
What ever became of those
Magnificent things…
Clearly you blocked the
Incident from your mind;
For those "magnificent" ear pieces
Never made it past
The morning sunrise
Outside Budapest,
After you introduced them -
Forcefully -
To the gravel-covered earth.

It makes me chuckle;
The image in my mind,
And your puzzled questioning
To this day!

– Tech Frustrations

Time is wearing thin
As work begins to beckon;
A question of our return
Upon their invisible lips.

I do not wish to be reminded,
I do not wish to be dragged back -
Mentally
Nor physically -
To a life of 'normality'
And odd pretending.

But you too
Have a limit on your time;
Your job also awaits you -
Though yours is more exciting than mine!

So it is with great reluctance
Within my soul
That we blitz our way through
Austria, Germany and Belgium,
Causing them to blur
And blend
To become as one.

It is difficult to differentiate
Happenings,
Villages,
Or scenery,
During those last days on the road;
Although there is one uplifting memory
Of an early morning start

Róisín Taylor

In Germany
Where the sky was filled with
Colorful balloons
To lift our spirits, for the journey home.

– *Time's a-Ticking*

Perched upon our metal steed,
Who carried us across
This continent -
Oftentimes safely,
Only rarely did you falter
Or abruptly throw
Us from you.

Even then,
You were gentle
And we undamaged;
You were always ready for the off
Once we had gathered ourselves
Together.

Your burnt, orange body
Shone in the afternoon sun,
Never once overheating,
Always ready
For the road
Without hesitation.

Our wonderful Varrie -
You did so well,
To carry us from
Country to country
Without complaint;
I know you still would
If we asked it of you again.

– Varrie

So many impressions
Stored away -
Kept safe -
Everyday a new adventure,
Within this mighty journey.
Photos cannot do you justice;
They cannot capture
Your likeness,
The feelings, thoughts,
Nor the context
Of all of these moments
That together add-up,
Creating this grand,
And dizzying
Experience.

– The Difficulties of Capturing You

Of course there were naysayers
When we announced our plan!
They didn't think I would last;
Believed that I would
Trade beautiful Varrie
For a creature of metal wings,
To fly above the earth at
Opportunities first showing,
Abandon ship after short words
Or rising tempers.

I laugh now,
As I laughed then,
You see
They forgot the most important factor:
I am my father's daughter;
My stubbornness stems from him!

– Like Father, like Daughter

I had this odd obsession,
Borne from you
I believe,
To calm my breaking heart,
To still my flowing eyes,
To turn such sad sights
Into something intriguing;
Those still, lifeless forms
Splayed out by the
Deadly roadside,
All fur and awkwardly broken -
Less red than expected,
But dead all the same.

You would stop,
Every time,
And help me complete
Their journey;
Small hand lost within yours,
We would leap,
Times three,
Over these unfortunate creatures;
For luck
You informed me,
For their memory.

My soul comforted,
For some way to explain
The reasons why
My heart drummed,
But mostly
To acknowledge a life ended;
To understand the fragility

Of it all
And give respect to death
No matter the creature it came for.

A powerful teaching,
Regardless of your intention
Or reasonings;
It resonated with me deeply,
Creating a mind of curiosity
And - in a sense - of nonconformity.

And so, when we took on Europa,
I had a need to capture
Those silent forms
And send them safely
On their way
Whilst their memory shall
Live as I live;
They showered us in luck
As we explored
Each magnificent country -
Every creature found
And freed -
Like a ritual
Wrapping around us protectively
To deliver us home safe
And in one piece.

– Rituals and Obsessions

What a privilege it was
To explore this continent
With you,
A magnificent experience indeed.

An adventure made special -
Unique -
Because we took it on
Together;
Father and daughter
And the ever faithful
Varrie:
Our 1999 Honda Varadero,
Majestic and proud.

Five weeks of exploring
Europa,
Thirteen flags collected
In our pockets;
Sights that have been
Burned into my mind
Still clear as day
Should I wish to look upon them again.

An incredible journey
To say the least -
I believe it's time that
We plan the next one!

– Exploring Europa

Éire

A land so full of magic,
It's a wonder
That it is not embraced more
By Her people.

Up to our eyes in thick,
Fantastical mythology;
Neolithic remains littering
The lush landscape
Begging to be understood.

The old ways have fallen
On deaf ears
As the age of technology
Tramples over our senses,
Leaving us numb,
Empty,
And longing.

I feel the soft buzz
Of the land
So eager to erupt;
Covering us with heroes
And majestic creatures
Once again.

But what would the legends of old have to say
Of this new world?
Would the mighty Queen of Connaught
Still fight for her bull?
How about the fierce Queen of the Sea,
Would she still sail into palaces fearlessly?
And what of the Ard Rí Himself?

Would he step up to claim
The fallen Hill?
Would the Other Crowd
Be capable of enticing us away
From our beloved devices
With their whimsical music,
Their hypnotic dance,
And tainted wine?
Would they even want to?

This world has moved away from
Myths and legends,
Forgotten are the gateways
And rituals.
The land lies dormant now,
Deep within its slumber,
Protected from our modern insanity.

But it shall forever hold the truth;
This mystical land
Will never forget,
For it holds them tight,
Keeping them safe,
Until the time is right
To release these wonders
Back into the world.

– Éire

Róisín Taylor

Through the rocky terrain
I wander with loyal companion in tow,
Running soundlessly,
Without aim, mission or goal;
He stalks.

Sure-footed and keen-eyed,
The way forward is up,
Over and around -
Like life -
Towards the sky
And all its beauty and secrets.

Delicate wings fluttering by,
Speckled with golden-brown and grey,
Blending in with the age-old green;
Where they go,
Where they lay,
Is a mystery beyond my reach.

Obstacles to overcome are plentiful
In this contrasting land
Of life and rock;
They merge to become one,
The same, beautiful,
Reclaiming what is Hers -
A home for all to seek.

Embraced by the warmth of life,
A mild autumn breeze rustling
The fallen leaves
As we pass by unnoticed
Upon the knife-edge

Of a sharp and unforgiving cliff;
Flat of face,
Who only few can read.

Beasts, both large and small,
Graze lazily.
Without boundaries -
Without signs -
Gracefully they stand tall
Amongst the twisted, ancient trees;
Wise in their ways
And in their eyes.

Flowers which were once scattered throughout,
Vibrant and alive meer weeks past,
Now brittle and falling back
Into their slumber
To sleep till it is time to rouse
Once more;
Bringing this seemingly barren land
Back to life.

So where does one choose to wander
In this place so full of life and death,
Beauty and harshness,
Energy and wonder?
Wherever you wish -
Whenever you wish -
For it will find you,
As you find it.

– Life Within the Mysterious Burren

Holy Mountain of the West,
Made so by he
Who ousted the Old Ways
To replace them with a
Shiny new one...

Holy Mountain shrouded in mist,
Your summit hidden in a
Thick blanket of white -
How symbolic -
Eluding me at every uphill turn,
With loose rocky path
Slipping away from under my feet.

I push on regardless,
Regardless of the sideways rain
And battering wind
Trying in vain to push me back,
Howling in exposed ears:
You shall not conquer me,
Oh wandering soul.

I push on,
Laughing at the rain,
Welcoming the breeze;
Respecting this Mountain of mist
As she throws nature herself at me -
Do you not realise,
She is with me always?
I am within her playground we fondly
Call home.

I am at peace with her,
And so this wind becomes an embrace,

The rain leaves me refreshed,
And the voice turns into encouragement -
Urging me on -
Pushing me up topless slopes,
As they fade into the clouds.

I dread the return,
The eventual tedious journey down,
But the whispering wind now
Kisses my face
With words that can never be words,
And with it
All worry vanishes from my being.

Mountain of mist -
Holy Mountain of the West -
I embrace this struggle,
I respect your might -
I will prevail!
Not for a faith
Which leaves me cold;
For you were here long before they -
You were here before all,
You are true
And far deeper.

I push on,
For your truth.
I pass by pilgrims of all ages,
Bent over double
As they too make their way up
Treacherous paths,
Their faces painted with rich focus,

And determination;
A fire burning within their very eyes.

The mist grows thicker now,
Closer to the top,
The small white church lost from view;
Revealing itself only when I am by its side -
Sheltering from the new onslaught
Of aggressive wind,
It wants us all gone,
Perhaps testing us to see if we have
What it takes to stand tall
And firmly
Upon the summit of this
Mountain of clouds.

Resting weary legs
I reflect
And conclude;
There can be no conquering achieved
Of a mountain,
Only prevailing and respecting.

How can one truly expect
To conquer Earth by
Simply claiming so?
No. There is no conquering here,
Only acceptance,
That these lands -
This mountain -
Shall outlive us all
And know not of our passing;
Accept this and move on,
She whispers softly from the mist.

Descending,
I glide effortlessly,
Sidefaced.
Focussed and exhilarated,
I am guided down,
Sure of foot;
My dancing feet find solid rock
To hold my form.
The wind no longer fights me;
Instead it surrounds me,
Keeping me upright
And yet pushing me smoothly onwards -
Like a friend of old -
I have no fear of falling now
And so I do not.

The hidden sun rises higher,
Slowly burning away the mist,
And as low clouds drift off,
Blue can be seen
Above and below;
Sea and sky reflecting one another.
I smile and hum my thanks
As I steadily flow my way to the base
Of this former mountain of mist -
A formidable foe,
A loving friend,
Nature's teacher to the core;
It has been a pleasure
Learning from you today.

– Mountain of Mist(ery)

Prague

Róisín Taylor

A mighty, long weekend away,
Just you and me;
Gobbling up the mysteries,
Histories and beauties
Of the picturesque city
That is Prague.

Streets roamed for hours,
Intricate clock tower
Watched and watched again,
With wonder and mulled wine.

Your birthday celebrated
With food and laughter,
Mother's day with wine and
A quick hello to your god,
And International Women's Day
With deep red roses
Gifted to us from our favorite waiter,
In that delicious restaurant
We just couldn't seem to leave.

A jam-packed four days,
Indeed;
How I long to steal you away
Again.
Soon, Mother mine,
Soon.

– Celebrating You

Strolling through this City,
So magic and majestic;
Caught in the whirlwind of beauty,
We walk with shining eyes
That smile pure delight
As they take in the wonderment of it all.

Delights squashed into six hours –
Our poor feet –
We feast on it all with hungry eyes,
Focused for more,
Eyes wider, then blinking
To store away the memories.

We pass by decades in a heartbeat,
Centuries in a footfall,
Generations with a breath,
In this City of ancient bafflement and monarchy.

To have experienced it all with you, dearest Mother,
Is memory enough for me.
I'd do it all again with you in the morning –
With our runaway bags and money.

– City of Memories

Thailand, Laos & Vietnam

After listening to years of you raving
About your tropical second home
In the sun,
Drenched in humidity
And sparkling clear waters;
I finally went along with you -
As your bag lady,
Helping you to cart the equipment
Of your dreamings -
To follow fighters
And document thrills.

I don't think I really knew
What to expect
Of this land of temples,
Islands, disorder
And bottomless buckets -
Certainly I did not expect
To fall so hard
And so fast
For the chaotic beauty
As I did;
As you must have done
All those years ago
Upon your very first visit.

A month we moved around
This delightful land,
Experiencing plenty
And learning even more;
It was this trip,
I believe,
That brought us closer,

Dear brother,
As we witnessed
Our similarities
Shining through the differences
And laughed at each other's madness,
Pushing each other's buttons
Without ever causing a fight.

I learned of your obsession -
Your unconditional love
And need
For pillows -
As you stacked them around you
With a contented, cheeky smile.

And you discovered a fear
Of my feet
At the end of a long, hot
And sweaty day!
I revelled in that realisation
As you dry-heaved
Between bursts of laughter.

You brought me to your favorite places,
Introduced me to your
Collection of friends
Who wrapped me in warm welcomes
And enticed me to stay.

I think I understand you better now;
Why it is you return so often
To this disorganised paradise,
With its smiling, sleepy people,

Warm seas
And endless possibilities.

It won your heart
And captured your soul,
Which I'm sure you gave up willingly -
I know this
Because I fear,
That I have now done the same.

– *Thai Brother*

When my chest feels squeezed by an
Unseen iron grip,
The sudden realisation that my body and
Soul are separated from one another
And I long for a reunion -
To return.

The feeling of stagnation staggers me,
Knocking me back mentally…
always mentally!
Memories of cycling in Chiang Rai,
On a sunny February morn;
The welcoming breeze whipping
Through my mane,
Wild and free -
Like my soul -
As I cruise down country lanes and
Beaten tracks, and up
Temple hills;
For a 'nosey' of course.

No map, no navigation,
Just straight up adventuring,
Trusting my dodgy directional senses!

The sun, reaching his peak,
Sparkles upon the river,
Ever moving, flowing,
They dance together
In the edges of my eye,
As I sigh with a longing to
Dance alongside them;
But I have yet to learn their dance -

Intricate and intimate as it is
And so I admire and smile,
Pure bliss flowing through my life streams.

If ever I need inner peace
This is where I go -
Should you need to find me -
I return
In my mind of dreams
I am cycling
Cycling in Chiang Rai.

– Chiang Rai Cruising

Koh Tao,
What can I say?
I adore you,
I am at peace within your inviting embrace,
In love and at one with you.

I have danced in your tears of joy
As the heavens opened,
Swam within your warm sea of life
And became a mermaid upon your rocks;
A tiny fish in your vast, glorious waters.

We may have had our ups and downs -
But what relationship hasn't?
Even with bandaged leg -
The legendary 'tourist tattoo' -
I danced with joy and strangers alike
And swang on ocean swings.

So I shall keep you in my heart
Always
And forever more.

Koh Tao, I thank you!

– Koh Tao, with Love

Róisín Taylor

The impressive Lamprayha will leave
You weak -
A shaking version of yourself -
A newborn
Propped up on wobbling legs.

It will cause your stomach to heave
Along with the unrelenting waves,
As the Lamprayha smashes through
Each and every swell.

One might contemplate the sanity of ever
Leaving the safety of idyllic shores
To encounter such a journey…
Surely it's not worth it?!

Perhaps this is why so many
Extend their stay…
It is not the tropical bays,
The thrilling drives,
Nor the deep, soulful peace that keeps us;
No,
It's not your decision to make;
It's the Lamprayha,
She will make you stay.

– The Lamprayha Decides

Gentle and hypnotic,
As you lap against rock and sand,
Ebbing and flowing;
Such peace from one so powerful.
I am fascinated by you
And your might.
Wash over me -
Leave me bare -
To start afresh;
A new life, by a new sea.
Same same, but different…
Or so they say.

– Same Same

Róisín Taylor

Swaying gently upon patient currents,
Lazily delivering us to our destination,
In no great rush as you meaner down
The Mekong River;
With twists a plenty
And sights of beauty,
I am in awe of you.

Flanked on one side of this slow
Wooden boat
Is the magical land of a thousand smiles;
A place that steals you away and
Tucks you safely into her embrace.
And on the other side
Is a new land waiting to be explored:
The land of a million elephants.

A two day journey
On a long slow boat packed tight
With locals and adventurers alike,
Their differences showing most clearly in the eyes;
There are those that shine,
Filled with excitement,
Afraid to blink out of fear of missing this passing new world,
Captivated by such beauty.

And then those that are used to such sights,
Just another day,
Another mode of transport,
Best to use this time for rest;
No longer are they fascinated by the scenery
Or by the tourists
Flooding into their lands
With cameras full of forgetful memories.

Rocking slightly down this river of life,
Dodging sharp teeth of exposed rocks;
Our carriage continues its course
As the Mekong River opens up
Revealing a wondrous valley
Of tall mountain peaks reaching
For the heavens,
Forestry and bamboo villages dotting their sides.

The water seems endless
As the sun bounces off its surface
Highlighting the bathing children playing;
Naked and shameless,
They wave frantically as we are carried on by.

Glimpses of golden-orange flash through gaps in the trees,
As the modest monks glide from nature into the villages,
Paying no more heed to us
Then the passing mountains do.

The deepening smile on my lips
Etches permanent lines into my skin,
Adding understanding and light to my eyes;
Enjoying the here and now -
As it should be.

— The Mekong River Teaches

Monday morning in mid-May, working 7-3 -
Doesn't quite have the same ring to it,
But it is what it is, and that's how it is…
For now.

10am: I've made 36 parts in two hours – go me.
Holding the fragile pieces delicately over a scalding heat gun;
I count away the seconds,

One…two…three…
And I slip away, yet again, to another vivid memory,
A wonderful experience,
A conversation,
A smell,
A taste…
I relive it all, sighing, as I make my 37th part.
I have been dragged back to this "reality"
Of which I have joined out of necessity…
And yet, willingly.

I feel half a person – present, but not quite in full –
Like the tales of old;
I have tasted the wonders of the Otherworld,
Now I am captivated, enthralled,
And somewhat incomplete -
Here in the flesh…but not in soul…
No, she dances freely in Vietnam,
Confused by my body's reckless abandonment,
She calls to me.

I could go to her, right now, but my purse draws its strings
About my carefree, exposed neck
Whispering, *"Not today girl, not today"…*

One…two…three…four…
I am in the mountains surrounded by fertile fields
And smiling faces,
Children waving and shouting, "Hello!" as we drive by.

Perhaps not today, purse of mine.
I'm on 40 now…I'm doing ok for half a person!

Five…six…seven…
Dining in the dark, my taste buds exploding,
As we laugh awkwardly with our visually impaired server.

Imagination allowing me to see in a very peculiar way –
I can find my glass of smooth red without any issue at all!
My body is being spoken to…
I smile and nod; I'm on 45…wow wee…!

Eight…nine…ten…
Using Google Translate to have a broken conversation
With a timid beauty sporting a fashionable snaggle tooth;
A sadness hidden deep behind that smile,
We connect – somehow – secret smile to secret smile,
The eyes never lie.
She fed us till we were fit to burst!

Perfectionism kicks in…the need to reach 100 parts by
the end of my shift;
Today's the day!

Ten…eleven…twelve…
Laughing uncontrollably in the sea,
The kind of laughter to chase away the dark,
Laughter to make you physically hurt with the sheer

hilarious violence of it!
Salty water filling my lungs and stomach
With each explosion of giggles,
We don't care, we are happy –
We're going for veggie burgers and a drive to the Red
Desert –
Happy travellers splashing about.

There are too many issues with the parts...
I have to stop counting parts now,
I must try to concentrate…
I need to reach 100 parts, focus girl!
But my mind slips away, controlled by forces unseen,
I care not.

Thirteen…fourteen…fifteen…
Buses, sleeper buses, trains, planes, bicycles, scooters,
motorbikes,
Boats, taxis and feet…
We made our way through this land that steals me away.
I close my eyes to open my mental third,
And there it is,
There we are,
There I am!
Grooving to the beats of unpredictable expectations,
Body and soul, hand in hand: whole.
We shall be reunited soon, soul of mine,
To start a new adventure…
Just six more months of counting the seconds,
Counting the parts;
Then I'm gone.

– Vietnam Daydreamer

I'm on the drunk side of tipsy;
I've been guzzling down life and
Cheap Vietnemese beer,
Surrounded by familiar faces - though
Still strangers by heart.
We attempt a game of pool in between
Fits of giggles
From the over filled balloons.

I dance with Bolinda
Who tells me to call her Bo -
Together we are RoBo! Unstoppable!
We neck shots of tequila
In honor of the barman's birthday
And to work up the courage -
The warmth -
To rid ourselves of pesky clothing
And take a dip
In the moonlit sea of Cát Bà.

My heart races with excitement and a hint of
Hiding anxiety;
Self conscious of my imperfectly perfect body.

Bo - this fantastical French woman -
Complements me offhandedly, candidly;
Not sexually
Nor was she objectifying,
Just one human complimenting a fellow human
And for once I am able to accept it
Without the bashfulness or shame
That often follows.

Hand in hand,
Laughing wildly
We run to greet the sea,
To dance once more
With gentle waves swaying with us.
Thank the gods for tequila
And for the magnificent Bolinda!

– Skinny Dipping in Cát Bà

Sweden

Róisín Taylor

From sun to snow,
Within ten and a half hours...
Strange the way the body adapts,
Reacts,
And accepts
What the mind is reluctant to grasp.

I was unprepared;
My summer wear inappropriate
For such crisp air
Upon exposed skin,
My breath enclosing around my face
In a white mist.

I trick myself against the onslaught of cold,
Invoking fresh memories of warmth
And the sun.
But this *is* magical,
This softly glowing whiteness
Blanketing all that it touches;
The air holds a freshness,
Banishing the impurities
Of a hot and humid day
Like those I've left behind.

I hungrily gulp down this clean air -
With a smile upon my blue lips -
While I cautiously tread across lakes
Frozen thick;
Blowing my mind!
This frozen wonderland -
Such a contrast to yesterday's world -
Surprises my body -

mind full of memories

Has me feeling renewed,
Refreshed,
And re-energised.

I am ready for this next adventure,
Ready for the next step…
Let's hope the ice will hold.

– From Sun to Snow

Turn back
They pleaded,
Too much snow
They preached,
Helicopter rescues
They warned.

Yet, forwards we continued,
Willing to risk it -
Stubborn minds set
With a "we're here now" attitude,
And anyways, the high summer sun
Spoke a different story;
Touching our faces with enough
Warmth to scare away
The remains of winter's bite
Blowing down from mountain tops.

Delicious icy springs
Act as a constant companion
Along this winding, earthy path,
Waiting to be scooped up
And drank -
Always there should we need it.

The first glance of your
Glistening white peaks
Robbed my lungs of their breath;
Rising proudly from luscious green meadows
And rushing rivers of life.

A 22-kilometer hike,
Passing base camp

To find a nook of our own to
Rest our weary bodies
Loaded with equipment.

We nestled into your valley;
Home to wild reindeer
And echos,
In a time of light
Where the sky forgets
The darkness
And the stars are a distant memory
Of the long winter passed.

Others take advantage
Of these never sleeping days;
Setting sights and feet to your summit
Late in the would-be evening.

Indeed a heavy snow had fallen
Mere days ago,
But the mountains shone
Their favour upon us
With a luminous sun skimming
The horizon
As we made our way,
Come the supposed morning,
To dance this magnificent beast
Of steep inclines
And breathtaking views,
Of hundreds of stone stackings
And a soul-shattering,
Monstrous
U-shaped valley

With loose rocks waiting for
Unsecure feet
To slide downwards
Towards a blanket of
Blinding snow;
The whiteness made more so
By the black-grey boulders
Joining us in our next ascent,
Touching the empty blue.

It seemed an age
To break free
Of the grey;
Snaking our way
Towards the sun,
Each ledge believed to be
The last
Just to be met with evermore grey.

Feet and knees crying out
With each careful step
We journey on
And up,
On…
And up.

When finally - suddenly -
The dreary grey
Is met with powder white
And your peak
Lies ahead;
Your gentle slope
Like a bent over giant

Frozen in time,
Wearing a grand coat
Of icy snow
Patiently waiting for the
All too short summer sun
To melt you free once again.

Until then
You sleep and graciously welcome
The tiny explorers
Who wish to conquer you.

Trudging through the deep snow,
We slowly edge our way -
Sun bouncing from the white,
Illuminating our delighted faces -
We make the final climb
To your beautifully formed
Summit;
Gasping at the heavens,
Taking in the glorious panorama
Of endless mountains,
Countless peaks,
And dizzying heights
With terrifying space between
Heaven and earth.

Gingerly,
I step out on to your narrow ledge,
For the customary snapshot;
Breath held within,
Knees going weak
And stomach churning with that
Peculiar feeling of fear mixed with adrenaline.

Gladly stepping away from
The void,
Allowing air to rush into my
Lungs
And my legs to buckle safely
Beneath me,
Falling softly into the snow.

Indeed, I may have stood atop
You, gentle giant,
But in no way does that
Make me your master -
Never was that my intention;
I humbly wished to
Gaze upon you,
Witness your power,
Your beauty,
And the beauty of your surroundings.

That wish you granted
A hundred times
And more.
Enjoy your peaceful slumber,
Sleeping giant,
Dream of dancing with the sun,
Laughing with the clouds,
And flirting with the moon
And her stars.

We shall make our way back down
To civilisation
With ecstatic bliss etched
Into our souls

And smiles upon our faces,
We bid you farewell…
For now.

– Climbing Kebnekaise

Sailing the Swedish Archipelago
From island to island;
Each one as exquisite as the last,
Becoming more and more difficult to depart
As each plot of heavenly earth
Captivates small portions of my soul.

We embrace our natural forms,
Roaming and swimming
Without a care;
Allowing the sun to kiss our skin
And the warm summer winds to dry us.

Ten glorious days
Of truly wonderful, magical adventures -
A gift I shall cherish
Until my last breath.

The warm, salty waters,
The gentle lapping of the sea,
And our four-legged Queen
Elated with her very first swim!

"A summer to remember";
That was my wish,
Before the soft autumn winds
Come to carry me away.

Indeed it has been just that,
And so much more;
These dreamlike sea days
Will surely be impossible to forget.

My appreciation is overflowing
Of this time
We have given to each other -
Memories of a lifetime
Condensed into three years.

And so, as we make our way
Back to main land,
Island hopping life still fresh upon our skin,
We accept the inevitable
And enjoy every last minute
That time gifts.

— Sailing on Borrowed Time

My dearest Anam Cara, soul queen,
Nature fairy!
Älskling,
Your friendship brought more than laughter
To my stardust collection.

My fellow woman of the sun,
Our trip to your island -
Your home -
Is one I shall hold protectively
Within my heart
Till it beats its last drum.

The stunning world of Gotland
Gave peace to my clattering mind,
As you joyfully led me
Around nature, castle
And the idyllic old town
Surrounded by a proud stone wall
Protecting the bustling life within;
Its shining stores of trinkets,
The blooming flowers creeping up
Quaint houses,
And ice cream of countless flavours!

Jumping on our rented scooter
We hit the road northbound
And east
To your delightful house nestled into
The countryside
By the shallow, clear sea.

We walked and swam,

Laughed and drank -
Such bountiful laughter we had my dear,
At silliness and madness,
At life and all its twists and bends.

I showed you the ways of the scooter -
Our two wheeled beauty,
Who outright refused
To go above 60km per hour -
But in truth
You were a natural
Like a tree to earth;
You took hold,
Fearless as ever,
Like a pro!

My time in the enchanting
Sverige
Would have been quite different
Had I not stumbled upon
A rare diamond
Such as you,
Mo anam cara -
My soul sister of nature -
Thank you for the adventure,
And for being the magical creature that you are!

— *The Importance of a Soul Sister*

Nepal & Sri Lanka

The Annapurna Circuit Saga:

3
Weeks of hiking

2
Traumatised feet

1
Poem per day

A lifetime of memories!

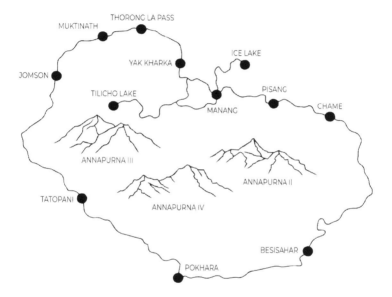

Illustration by Daniela Jarrín Sánchez

Annapurna Circuit: Day One
5th Oct 2018

Incredible, that feeling
Of experiencing different emotions
At the same time;
The overwhelming awes
Of the rising mountains,
The unbelievable sights
Of this strikingly beautiful country,
And the deafening screams
From the body and mind;
Aching and protesting.

At a point of near deliriousness -
With hardly a chance to catch
A breath -
I exhale "Wow"
Repeatedly,
The only way my over-exposed brain
Is able to express and release
All of these feelings
Into one
Exhausted sound...
Incredible that.

Annapurna Circuit: Day Two
6th Oct 2018

Two hours into this exquisite day,
My body and mind were in turmoil;
Right foot bearing the wounds
Of bubbling skin.

Each step rubbing,
Causing agony to shoot
From heel to mind;
Dulling the beauty of my surroundings.

Thankfully, I have patience by my side,
And together we adopt a slow walk,
Allowing breaks
And time to retie my leather boots.

As the day wore on
My foot grew numb
And I remembered
What it is to laugh.

With love alongside me
And the power of the mountains
To lull my thoughts into silence,
Allowing me to appreciate the astounding scenery
Within which I roam.

Annapurna Circuit: Day Three
7th Oct 2018

I feel stronger today,
Not just in my body,
But within my very soul.

I've stopped with the inner
Voicings of *"I can't"*
And have replaced them
With a kind of mantra
Of my own;
I will share it with you,
If you like:

I am capable.
I am able.
I am strong.

Each line for every
Gruelling uphill step -
A chant to chase away the negativity
Clouding my mind.

I can do this,
I am doing this!
Just you wait and see,
I will do this!

Annapurna Circuit: Day Four
8th Oct 1988-2018

I awoke to the sight of a lone snow capped
Mountain,
The first taste of what lies ahead.
Dawn slowly casting its light upon
The magnificent view;
A feeling created of fluttering excitement
Within the very pit of my form.

What a delicious way to start the day;
Especially on this day.
30 years since I fought,
Together with my mother -
Thanks to my mother -
To enter this life.
30 years of fighting
To remain strong,
To earn this life -
Live this life!

Today I continue this fight,
Pushing myself onwards
Through the ever changing terrain,
Each and every uphill struggle
Causing my heart
And my feet
To cry out in protest.

But my will;
My stubbornness -
Thanks to my father -

Only grows stronger.
30 years of hard lessons learned
Have made me
Who I am today...
I thank myself for dragging me to this point.

– Thirty Years in the Making

Annapurna Circuit: Day Five
9th Oct 2018

We went our separate ways today,
You venturing the upper lands
While I explore the lower.
And what a glorious day it was!
It was the trail my body yearned for;
To heal,
And develop.

The warm sun upon my foolishly
unprotected skin -
Hindsight is a bitch they say!
But oh, the valleys,
The rolling hills and
Sparkling white topped mountains,
Hugging me close
In their circular embrace;
My soul did weep
And my eyes forgot what blinking was;
Why would you ever do it?!

I loved today -
Everything about it -
I simply overflowed with love.
I sat when and where ever I wished,
No pressure to keep up with anyone,
Taking in all of the wondrous beauty
At my own steady pace.

Manang is in my pocket now,
I can rest here a while;

Acclimatise and wash my dusty hair!
Allow my body some peace,
Before taking on the next
Leg of this soul-filling journey.

Annapurna Circuit: Day Six
10th Oct 2018

You are steep and endless,
Each top an illusion
Met with another,
More arduous climb;
Zig zagging our way up
Your dizzying spine.

'Acclimatization day':
A trek which decides your fate,
Testing your blood of its levels.
Side missions like these
Will show you if you are worthy
Of the true heights still to come;
Many before me have had to turn back at this point.

But onwards we continue upon
Your dusty, snake-like path,
Up and up
And up..
Until suddenly you open up;
Showering us in your beauty,
My breath was stolen
Countless times this day.

The green-blue lakes,
Nestled atop your head -
Not iced, as your name would suggest -
Sparkled and flowed in the midday sun
As we sat and ate,
Drinking in the wondrous snowy mountains

That envelop us;
Blindingly white
And ever so slightly intimidating!

Alas, I fear
These words do you no justice -
No words truly can -
But I thought I'd better try.

Annapurna Circuit: Day Seven
11th Oct 2018

A holy Thursday -
The new day of rest -
Finally, my wounds can heal,
Relax
And prepare
For the intensity of the days to come.

Our family has grown;
From two to three,
Adopting our fourth
Atop the lake-filled mountain,
And stumbling into our fifth and sixth
Within the cosy interior
Of a Manang tea house.

My expanding mountain family
Of different nationalities,
Beliefs,
Desires,
And expectations;
Carried on the wind from scattered
Locations across the Earth.

We laugh together at the silly things,
And talk serious
Whenever seriousness is invoked.
And although our family
Is in its infancy,
Borne into reality mere days ago;
We take care of each other

And have each others' backs,
Whilst we wander the mountains
Of heaven together.

Annapurna Circuit: Day Eight
12th Oct 2018

I find that I am
Running out of ways to
Best describe the
Absolute splendour
Of this otherworldly place
Located in the sky.

The way is challenging,
Yet undoubtedly rewarding,
It does play tricks upon
One's fragile, exhausted mind
Turning my eyes a tainted green...
Perhaps, for a good reason;
For I witness you flirting
Openly - playfully - painfully.

I try my best
To focus on the beauty
Which surrounds me,
To remove you from
The foreground of my mind.
But it is only with healthy conversation
That I can truly move forward
To take in this slice
Of paradise
Without poison
Dripping
Into my mind
Obscuring the view.

Annapurna Circuit: Day Nine
13th Oct 2018

Fears were faced today,
Though, perhaps not yet conquered,
But certainly faced!
Walking upon narrow trails
With sloped, jagged mountain faces
Above me to my right,
And steep, sliding slopes
Below me to my left.

Heart stopping
Too many times to recall,
And my breath ceasing to be
As I tentatively stepped
Upon the loose, rocky sliver;
Stones falling free with each
Shaking step
Causing my heart to leap
Into my frozen throat.

Winding down treacherous declines
With feet losing grip
And body losing balance -
All I can see is the sudden, unprotected
Edge
As the path disappears around another boulder.

And my mind screams in vain;
My voice is nowhere to be found,
My body trembles uncontrollably,
Clinging to the safety of study rock

As I stop short of sliding off this
Insane path
With its landslide warnings.

But somehow, I made it through to the otherside
Of madness,
Eyes wide with terror
And soul traumatised by all too many close calls.

Indeed,
Fears were met on this day...
And will have to be met again.

– *The way to Tilicho Base*

Annapurna Circuit: Day Ten
14th Oct 2018

That water!
What can I say?
You must be the purest form of blue;
The blue all other blues
Are based on,
The kind of water all bodies of water
Aspire to be!

So still and peaceful,
You reflect the very heavens
You wish to touch,
Upon your surface.

With glaciers rushing to meet you
At your edges
And clumps of ice
Floating lazily within;
I admit
I have never seen a sight such as you.

My eyes drink you in,
Your icy breath
Reflecting in my own two blues.
You are stunning,
Spectacular,
And overwhelming
In every
Single
Way.

I would weep,
But your beauty is worth more
Than my tears;
You shall have my breath instead…
And my silent wish
To submerge my whole self
Within your tantalizing depths.

— Tilicho Lake

Annapurna Circuit: Day Eleven
15th Oct 2018

En route towards the Pass,
The highest in the world -
So they say -
At 5,416 meters,
The way is up
And then dramatically down;
My knees cry out
In protest for the days to come -
Despite my faithful poles
Taking the brunt of the impact.

My feet feel
As if I have been
Inappropriately wearing
Six-inch heels
Constantly
For the past week!

Three and a half hours hike
From base camp,
We have stopped -
Listening to our aching,
Hungry bodies -
At a stone tea house
Burrowed into the mountains,
To recuperate and prepare
For the world's highest pass.

Annapurna Circuit: Day Twelve
16th Oct 2018

It was you
Who was the fragile one
Last night;
Your body betraying you
As your stomach turned
And heaved.

I felt useless -
I wanted to take it from you,
Heal you of this
Torment.

But, selfishly,
I must admit
It was nice not to be the only
one suffering;
That feeling of being
"The weak one"
Finally not on me...
Terrible I know!
Yet I still would have taken it from you -
For you -
Had the sacrifice been offered.

For now though,
You must listen to your body
And rest,
As your mountain family waits
Patiently, glad of the pause
Before we move on
Once more.

Annapurna Circuit: Day Thirteen
17th Oct 2018

Sure,
You were a mental,
Emotional,
And physically demanding
Challenge;
With your never ending
Upwards slopes -
Your false illusions of
"This must be it...right?"
Wrong!

Sure,
You were all of those things,
And more,
But you are worth
Every mental cry,
Every disheartened uphill
And each and every
Psyching up for the next
Round of uphill battles.

Thorong La Pass,
Your endless valley of time,
Scattered with prayers
Blowing in your gusty breath;
It is far too soon to boast
That I would take you on again,
For I respect your might
And my feet still bleed tears
Of your all too fresh memory!

Annapurna Circuit: Day Fourteen
18th Oct 2018

My Heart!
My poor, soft,
Compassionate heart!
It poured over for you -
My four legged,
Wet-nosed,
Babe -
Tied to a pole
At the foot of a magnificent temple.

Watching with terror
As you witness the slaughter
Of another.

Blocking you from this
Nightmarish view
We spoke -
Secretly -
As I showered you
With as much love
As I have within me.

And I did weep
Great tears of helplessness
As your warm breath
Washed over my face;
Nose to nose.

Cried my love for you,
Cried for your fate.

It was in this moment
That I made a promise;
I love you too much
To eat you.

Annapurna Circuit: Day Fifteen
19th Oct 2018

We may have taken
A mountain bike route
With too many winding downhill tracks
And rocky paths,
But it showed us much
Beauty;
Like the idyllic stoney
Village of Lupra.

We walked upon
Wide, dried river bed
With monster cliff faces
Sheltering us from the
Unrelenting wind
That tried its hardest to
Pick us up and throw us back.

An unbelievably spectacular day
Of hiking
Ended with
The stark contrast of
A soul-deflating feeling
Brought on
After wandering into Jomsom…
A strange and eerie town
With hostile hotels
And a large military base.

The polar opposite
To the mountain villages

Who wrap you up in kindness and warmth.
It's no wonder so many choose to
Board a bus
Straight to Tatopani!

Annapurna Circuit: Day Sixteen
20th Oct 2018

Our day started out late
Because of a very special happening -
You see
We were all ill,
Rundown,
Energy tanks low.

We stopped before we got started
To have the first
Espresso coffee in over
Two weeks -
Our souls rejoiced!

When from nowhere;
From silence,
The quirky cafe bust into life,
As heartbreaking passion
Was transformed into music
Played upon piano, guitar and drum
By the owner and his friends.

Their energy lifted ours;
Scaring away the symptoms
Of our poor exhausted bodies.
Yes, we were behind schedule,
By a few hours..
But it was beyond worth it!

Every heartbeat drummed,
Every key struck,

Made the delay
An inspiration for the hike ahead.

— *The Sound of Coffee*

Annapurna Circuit: Day Seventeen
21st Oct 2018

How do I even go about
Explaining this day?
Kicked off with birthday celebrations
With homemade apple crumble
For breakfast,
Followed by woodland walks
And quaint villages
Lazily awaiting
The few wandering souls
Who have opted for feet
Over stomach-wrenching buses.

Sliding down non-existing paths
Swallowed up by landslides,
My head dizzy with fright
Of lost footing.

Crossing ice cold rivers
Barefoot;
My bandaged wounds
Frozen into silence.

A truly wonderful,
Terrifyingly ethereal day,
Ended perfectly with
Celebratory popcorn
Shared amongst our
Family of the Mountains.

Annapurna Circuit: Day Eighteen
22nd Oct 2018

The heat!
Oh the gruelling, unrelenting
Heat!
This lowland humidity
Suffocating me with every step.

I think back
To those days of bitterly cold mornings
And quickly changing clothes
In a panic not to get frostbite!
We wished for warmth then...
But this?
This heat
Mocks our foolish wishes with
Tormenting laughter.

My freshly healed face -
My poor burnt nose -
Has been forced back into
Hiding yet again
Within the stuffy confinements
Of my borrowed buff
As it contorts around my face
And over my head.

The track blends with the road,
Dusty and humming with traffic
The lower we descend.
Our chilly evening dreams
Of the fabled

Hot springs of Tatopani -
Turning rapidly into
Mind vomit
Just at the thought of it;
Our bodies drenched in sweat,
Hot water the last thing
We wanted…

For now
We want only to wash the road
From our minds and sleep a dreamless sleep.

Róisín Taylor

Annapurna Circuit: Day Nineteen
23rd Oct 2018

We are, all of us, feeling
A tad worse for wear
On this day;
Reluctant to move on,
Bodies aching
And yearning for peace.

A day of rest has been called...
And yet some of us cannot sit still,
For our souls still itch
And dream of adventure -
Even if it is just a small one.

Upon our mini excursion
We were welcomed
Into the humble home
Of two rooms,
Six sisters,
Two parents,
Grandparents
And a great grandfather;
Bundled together with happy smiles.

With ancient words
Of worship,
They blessed us individually,
Decorating our foreheads
With blood red powder and rice,
And entwining bundles of flowers
Into our hair.

Sharing food, strong spirits and
Laughter,
Words awkwardly translated by gestures
And shy smiles.

A random happening,
A powerful coincidence -
Certainly,
A magical day of rest.

Annapurna Circuit: Day Twenty
24th Oct 2018

Biting the bullet,
We made a decision
We had hoped not to make:
We booked passage on a jeep to Pokhara.

The final day of this exquisite adventure;
It is deeply upsetting
And yet surprisingly exciting.
Dust encrusted and cracking boots
Are no longer needed.
My feet
No longer needing bandages;
They can breathe easily now.

The navigation upon our phones
Estimated a two-hour journey
To our final destination…
The locals did not try to hide their laughter
When they say it will be six at the least!

The roads are treacherous;
The kind on which you would not expect to sleep,
Yet, exhilarating all the same.

I cannot help but smile and laugh
At the chaos,
Only to then be horrified by
The fresh landslide that occurred
Just moments before us,
Causing traffic to jam
And people to search the damage done.

Seven hours of bouncing;
Our young, experienced driver
Delivered us into Pokhara
Safe and in one piece.

Though our minds still spun
And reeled
And our balance out of whack,
It didn't take long for us to fall
For this beautiful lakeside city…
I fear it has already stolen us away.

Annapurna Circuit: October 2018

> Now has come our crossroads,
> The time to reflect
> Upon the simple fact
> That soon
> Our Mountain Family
> Must float our separate ways.
> Like the fallen leaves,
> We are set adrift
> To dance alone with the autumn breeze
> Into the weird and wonderful
> Unknown.

– Farewell to our Mountain Family

*For my Mountain Family that was thrown together
upon the incredible Annapurna Circuit: Johan Collin,
Ann-Christine (Annie) Weber, Jonathan (Jono) Handforth,
Aaron Babbitt and Bryden Bowley. Thank you all for being you.*

By the turquoise sea,
With but 3 days left
Of this incredible adventure,
I ponder over the past 2 months:

Nepal,
My love,
You were the most exquisite
Of explanations;
Your people
The rarest of diamonds
Nestled into the very
Mountains of heaven.
A joy purer than your mountain air,
You were - are - authentic
In every way.
The memories of your beauty
Are forever forged into my mind
Tattooed in the most intricate designs.

Sri Lanka,
My confused, exhausting, yet beautiful
Game of tug of war;
I fear I could not truly
Relax within you.
Falling ill twice,
I could not face
Your flavoursome rice and curries,
Your deep-fried spices,
Endless amounts of white breads
And sliced up papaya!
Despite being followed, groped and leered at,
However,

I witnessed honesty and helpfulness
Shining through.
Travelling your stunning countryside
Has been thrillingly jaw dropping,
Spectacularly terrifying
And wonderful.

But still,
Although enjoying your tropical waters
I know, truly,
That my heart and soul
Resides in Nepal,
In her immense
And powerful
Mountains.

– Mountains and Oceans

Scotland, England & Wales

2019,
Ten years since our last adventure -
How time does pass so rapidly -
We joined once again
To explore
And to witness the
Mystical allure of the
Scottish Highlands.

It may not have taken a whopping five weeks
This time round,
But we surely made the most of
Our precious time,
Reminding ourselves to stop
Often
To truly take it all in.

With advanced technology
Condensed into pocket-sized devices;
We snapped our memories
Not just of the wonders of
Hills and locks,
But of us both
Together
Enjoying this journey -
This life.

We got lucky with the weather -
Even when it rained
It did so magnificently,
Causing the world to shift
Dramatically -
Its colours bursting into life,

Creating moody scenes of cloud
Shrouded hills and crumbling castles
Disappearing into dark waters.

I lost count of the locks
Who called to me,
Enticing me to submerge my form
Within their icy depths -
To reside with them
Forevermore -
A tempting invitation for my airy soul
So in love with water.

Yet the earth holds firm to my itching feet,
There are safer waters to be swam in,
She whispers, understanding the
Alluring, fiery ways of the Other Crowd.

Its is hard to believe
Ten years have passed,
When it seems like only yesterday
We roamed the roads of
Europa.

And now we explore
The wild landscape of Scotland
Together again -
Upon a new beast;
Our peppy Africa Twin…
Perhaps a foreshadowing
Of adventures to come?

— *Wild Highlands*

My romantic soul,
Worried and distressed,
Heart swollen and tender,
Was filled with apprehension
When the wind delivered me
To London.

And yet
Nature finds me
In this city of mazes,
Huge and overpopulated;
Ever moving,
Never sleeping -
Constant -
And yet
She is here too,
As She promised She would be.

When I go in search of Her
She shows herself to me.
With open arms
And melting embrace,
She envelopes me in peace,
Silencing the deafening noise
From deep within.

– Nature's Promise

Even with freshly wounded heels
And deeply, aching legs,
I look upon this time
With a smile.

Hiking the alluring peaks of the
Brecon Beacons,
With but a few days notice -
A last minute 'seize the day'
Trip into nature!

A necessary impulsive decision
For us both,
I believe;
Worries, stress and anxiety
Melted away by gentle touch,
And blasted aside by nature's force
As we stood upon a cliff ledge -
Wind whipping and clawing,
Warning not to get too close -
Staring out at the lush greens below
And the startling blues above;
Such tantalising sights
And terrifying heights
Devoured eagerly whilst I prepare
Hot brews to chase away the
Cold fingers of heaven's breath.

I am grateful for your company,
A friendship rediscovered;
Blossoming into honey,
Rich and oh so sweet.

My mind emptied -
I am at peace -
With laughter in our souls
And compassion in our hearts;
We grabbed this opportunity,
Pushed each other on,
Soaked up every drop of beauty
That unfolded before us,
And breathed a sigh of relief
As this city-life detox
Successfully stripped us back to nature.

– Seize the Day

Epilogue

I fell into a journey
Of the most spectacular of places
Filled with reflections,
Vibrations
And revelations.

There is no concept of race,
No need for religion,
Money,
Fear,
Nore is there desire for possessions.

A place where sexuality is not identity,
Weakness nor stigma;
This is a place of the soul,
To wander in peace.

It has no need for flirtations of the skin,
No necessity to cling to faith
Other than the faith in oneself.
A place where the soul can be expressed
Without judgment,
Harassment
Or interruption.

A place for the soul
To be -
Just be-
To love and be loved,
To exude love in its purest,
Unconditional
Form.

A place like no other;
A journey so significant,
So opening,
That your soul will weep,
Giving birth to
Universes of peace,
Worlds of love,
And civilisations of truth.

A journey of a lifetime
And surprisingly
Closer than you might think.

— Inward Journey

About the Author

Róisín is an Irish poet, raised wild in the countryside and now lives with her partner, Matty (and not enough plants) in London. She began writing poetry whilst living on the west coast of Ireland in the buzzing, pocket-sized village of Doolin, Co. Clare. Inspired by nature and a lover of people-watching, she could get lost in the beauty of the simple things in life. Having lived and moved around Ireland for many years she was in need of a new challenge and so she moved to Stockholm, Sweden in 2018. There her love and passion for writing blossomed as she soaked up the Scandinavian nature on her doorstep for two and a half years.

Her love for adventure was encouraged and nourished during her childhood; growing up in the lush greenness of the Irish countryside with many places to lose and find yourself. It is no surprise that this sense of adventure stayed with her to the present day, as she explores life and all its beauty and torment.

In January of 2021 she set herself a goal: to write a book before the end of the year. It was obvious to her what her first book would be. Adventure Poetry.

Find her online
Instagram: @roisin_taylor_poetry
FaceBook: @taylorpoetry

Acknowledgements

I would like to thank everyone who made this book come into being, be it by words of encouragement, constant reminders and firm pushing, or actually being by my side on these incredible journeys.

To my delightfully mad family, for always supporting my wandering and believing in my dreams. For the journeys we took and the ones still to come. For the lessons learned and the wisdom passed down. For allowing and pushing me to be whoever and whatever I wanted to be.

To my dearest, most loyal friend, Chris Lock. Always my number one fan, no matter what creative path I found myself exploring; you always cheered me on. Your continual persistence of positivity towards my poetry has allowed me to believe!

This book would not have taken form without the excellent talent and enthusiasm of the four women who worked on it with me: my wonderful Editor, Joyce Challis, who did a wonderful job of deepening the flow of my work. I'm very lucky to have found you! To Katarina Nskvsky for the absolutely stunning cover design, and putting up with my indecisiveness! Daiana Vanesa Marchesi, for formatting and designing the interior. And to Daniela Jarrín Sánchez, for the map illustration design. Without each of you, this would not be the book that it is today!

And of course, my deepest thanks to my wonderful partner Matty, for without your generosity, patience and belief I truly feel I would have continued to put this project on the long finger forever! Your powerful words of advice are the reason I finally started this project. I am eternally grateful to you and everyday I am thankful that our paths crossed more than once in this life.

Last, but never least, to all those wandering souls I met along the way, Thank you! Keep wandering, keep exploring, maybe we'll meet again some day!

Printed in Great Britain
by Amazon